Especially for: _____

From: _____

_____

You're the Best Kind
of Friend

Artwork by
CLAIRE
STONER

HARVEST HOUSE PUBLISHERS

EUGENE, OREGON

You're the Best Kind of Friend

Text copyright © 2008 by Harvest House Publishers
Published by Harvest House Publishers
Eugene, Oregon 97402
www.harvesthousepublishers.com

ISBN-13: 978-0-7369-2273-9

Artwork designs are reproduced under license © 2008 by Claire Stoner, and may not be reproduced without permission. For more information regarding the use of this artwork, contact:

Claire's Studio LLC
Two Jefferson Court
New Freedom, Pennsylvania 17349
www. ClairesStudioLLC.com

Design and production by Garborg Design Works, Savage, Minnesota

Harvest House Publishers has made every effort to trace the ownership of all poems and quotes. In the event of a question arising from the use of a poem or quote, we regret any error made and will be pleased to make the necessary correction in future editions of this book.

Scripture quotes are taken from the HOLY BIBLE, NEW INTERNATIONAL VERSION®. NIV®. Copyright©1973, 1978, 1984 by the International Bible Society. Used by permission of Zondervan. All rights reserved; and from The Message. Copyright © by Eugene H. Peterson 1993, 1994, 1995, 1996, 2000, 2001, 2002. Used by permission of NavPress Publishing Group.

Printed in China

10 11 12 13 14 15 / LP / 10 9 8 7 6 5 4 3 2

Two are better than one,

  because they have a good return

for their work: If one falls down,

  his friend can help him up.

THE BOOK OF ECCLESIASTES

3

True friendship is
a knot that angel
hands have tied.

Other blessings may be taken away, but if we have
acquired a good friend by goodness, we have a blessing
which improves in value when others fail.

WILLIAM ELLERY CHANNING

Alone we can do so
little; together we can
do so much.

HELEN KELLER

There is no distance too far between friends,
for friendship gives wings to the heart.

KATHY KAY BENUDIZ

It was from you that I first learned
to think, to feel, to imagine, to believe.

JOHN STERLING

The best way
to mend a broken
heart is time
and girlfriends.

GWYNETH PALTROW

The glory of friendship is not
the outstretched hand, nor the
kindly smile, nor the joy of
companionship; it is the spiritual
inspiration that comes to one
when he discovers that someone
else believes in him and is willing
to trust him with
his friendship.

RALPH WALDO EMERSON

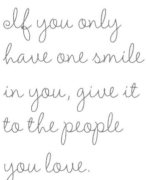

If you only
have one smile
in you, give it
to the people
you love.

MAYA ANGELOU

8

The biggest adventure you can take is to live the life of your dreams.

OPRAH WINFREY

No love, no friendship can cross the path of our destiny without leaving some mark on it forever.

FRANCOIS MAURIAC

Blessed are they who have
the gift of making friends, for
it is one of God's best gifts.
It involves many things,
but above all, the power of
going out of one's self, and
appreciating whatever is
noble and loving in another.

Thomas Hughes

Sometimes our light goes out but is blown into flame
by another human being. Each of us owes deepest
thanks to those who have rekindled this light.

Albert Schweitzer

Someone like you makes the heart seem the lighter,
Someone like you makes the day's work worth while,
Someone like you makes the sun shine the brighter,
Someone like you makes a sigh half a smile.
Life's an odd pattern of briers and roses,
Clouds sometimes darken, nor sun shining through,
Then the cloud lifts and the sunlight discloses
Near to me, dear to me——Someone like you.

Someone like you who stands steadfastly near me,
Knows me and likes me for just what I am,
Someone like you who knows just how to cheer me,
Someone who's real without pretense or sham.
Someone whose fellowship isn't a fetter
Binding my freedom——who's loyal all through,
Someone whose life in this world makes it better,
Blest to me, best to me——Someone like you.

Never a trouble but you help me bear it,
Just by the fellowship you have with me,
Never a joy but I want you to share it,
How far you fare or wherever you be.
Never a burden but you make it lighter
Just by your smile that I see creeping through,
Never a glad hour but you make it brighter,
Heart of me, part of me——Someone like you.

How come the thoughts of you joyously welling
Up like the water of springs bubbling clear,
What a new joy every time in the telling
Something that always I want you to hear.
Roses of June or the snows of December
Gray be the skies or like azure the blue,
Far be the day that I may not remember,
Near to me, dear to me——Someone like you.

James W. Foley

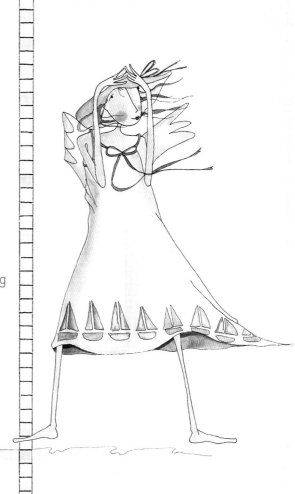

A friend loves at all times. THE BOOK OF PROVERBS

Let no one ever come to you without leaving better and
happier. Be the living expression of God's kindness: kindness
in your face, kindness in your eyes, kindness in your smile.

MOTHER TERESA

We cannot tell the precise moment when a friendship is formed. As in filling a vessel drop by drop, there is at last a drop which makes it run over; so in a series of kindness there is at last one which makes the heart run over.

JAMES BOSWELL

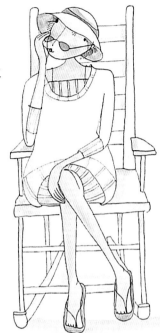

He who sows courtesy reaps friendship, and he who plants kindness gathers love.

SAINT BASIL

A kind heart is a fountain of gladness, making everything in its vicinity freshen into smiles.

WASHINGTON IRVING

If I planted a flower every time
I thought of you, I could walk
in my garden forever.

AUTHOR UNKNOWN

Friendship without self-interest is one of the rare and beautiful things of life.

JAMES F. BYRNES

Sweet souls around us! watch us still,
   Press nearer to our side;
Into our thoughts, into our prayers,
   With gentle helpings glide.

HARRIET BEECHER STOWE

All love that has not friendship for its base, is like a mansion built upon the sand.

ELLA WHEELER WILCOX

A friend is somebody you want to be around when you feel like being by yourself.

BARBARA BURROW

I think there is something wonderful about everyone, and whenever I get the opportunity to tell someone this, I do.

MARY KAY

Be good
friends who
love deeply

THE BOOK OF ROMANS

Friends are an aid to the young, to guard them from error;
to the elderly, to attend to their wants and to supplement
their failing power of action; to those in the prime of life,
to assist them to noble deeds.

ARISTOTLE

$\mathcal{R}$emember,
we all stumble,
every one of us.
That's why it's
a comfort to go
hand-in-hand.

EMILY KIMBROUGH

A good exercise
for the heart is to
bend down and
help another up.

JOHN ANDREW HOLMES JR.

Some of the most rewarding and beautiful moments of a friendship happen in the unforeseen open spaces between planned activities.

CHRISTINE LEEFELDT

I do not wish to treat friendships daintily, but with the roughest courage. When they are real, they are not glass threads or frost-work, but the solidest thing we know.

RALPH WALDO EMERSON

A friend is what
the heart needs
all the time.

HENRY VAN DYKE

God never loved me in so sweet a way before.

'Tis He alone who can such blessings send.

And when His love would new expressions find,

He brought thee to me and He said—"Behold a friend."

AUTHOR UNKNOWN

Friends...they cherish one another's hopes. They are kind to one another's dreams.

HENRY DAVID THOREAU

To be capable of steady friendship or lasting love, are the two greatest proofs, not only of goodness of heart, but of strength of mind.

WILLIAM HAZLITT

I'd like to be the sort of friend
that you have been to me;

I'd like to be the help that
you've been always glad to be;

I'd like to mean as much to you
each minute of the day

As you have meant, old friend
of mine, to me along the way.

EDGAR A. GUEST

*Father, thank
You for putting
into my life the
dear friends that
add so much
sunshine. Amen.*

AUTHOR UNKNOWN

Thanks for the sympathies that ye have shown!
Thanks for each kindly word, each silent token,
That teaches me, when seeming most alone,
Friends are around us, though no word be spoken.

HENRY WADSWORTH LONGFELLOW

A man of many companions may come to ruin, but there is a friend who sticks closer than a brother.

THE BOOK OF PROVERBS

Two things upon this changing earth can neither change nor end;
The splendor of Christ's humble birth, the love of friend for friend.

AUTHOR UNKNOWN

My friends have made
the story of my life.
In a thousand ways
they have turned my limitations
into beautiful privileges,
and enabled me to walk serene
and happy into the shadow
cast by my deprivation.

HELEN KELLER

Oblige with all your soul that friend
who has made a present of his own.

Socrates

O friend, my bosom said,

Through thee alone the sky is arched.

Through thee the rose is red;

All things through thee take nobler form,

And look beyond the earth,

The mill-round of our fate appears

A sun-path in thy worth.

Me too thy nobleness has taught

To master my despair;

The fountains of my hidden life

Are through thy friendship fair.

RALPH WALDO EMERSON